I0086550

SALEM

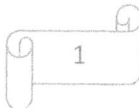

Create space printing press.

The Book of Salem.

PRINTED IN THE UNITED STATES OF AMERICA.

www.BlacksandLatinos.net

Twitter.com/EzraMicaiah

Facebook.com/BlacksandLatinos

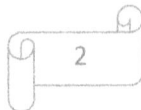

SALEM

A Light House

&

A City on a Hill

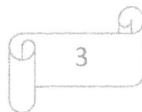

Twitter: @EzraMicaiah

BIOGRAPHY:

Ezra Micaiah Ben Israel born William Mckinley Veasley in 1992 in Houston, Texas United States of America. Born into this world a slave. Not free from the curses of my forefathers, but instead running the streets of Houston. Searching, pleading for a way out of poverty. Selling my soul to make a dollar and furthermore to fit in. Following illusions until one day a prophet of the God of Israel caught hold of me and spiritually body slammed me by the way. Afterwards picking me up and setting me in order, I rose up and stood upon my feet Ezra Micaiah Israel of the nation of Israel from the tribe of Judah. A student of Jesus Christ the black messiah, the Lion of the tribe of Judah, the root of David.

Shalom.

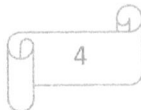

Table of Contents:

A Light House

A City on a Hill

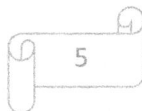

Introduction:

This book is not to be mated with
The Holy Bible in any way shape
Or form. The bible is the
Only one hundred percent true
Book on the face of the earth, nor
Can any other book be mated
With it. I am only a student
Of Christ and the Prophets.
Inspiration for this book came
From the Bible.
Chapters do not have one topic,
Many have multiple topics.

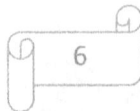

SALEM:

<u>A Lighthouse</u>

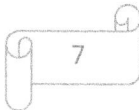

Chapter One

I.   This is the purgetero, the path to paradiso, through the inferno ending at Salem.

II.   Herein lye the way of belief in the unseen: but that which is the more evident.

III.   The way of faith, and the path of the believing.

IV.   From everlasting unto everlasting dwelt faith: and unto all eternity shall she abide.

V.   She cometh before manifestation:
as lightning goeth forth before
thunder.

VI.   She shall be after manifestation:
as the righteous that shall spring
forth after the wicked.

VII.   By her jewels were created: and
by her rubies were found.

VIII.   And as iron sharpeneth iron: so
doth faith strengthen faith.

Chapter Two

I. One was once blind and now he seeth: and one was once dead and now he liveth.

II. Lethargy hath compassed the sons of God: and hell has not released her captives.

III. Man hath awoke from the lethargy like one off strong drink.

IV. And so, let's begin.

V. I beheld that which was around me and discerning among them, I wondered greatly.

VI. What medicine is there of all the earth that can compare unto the medicine of the Most High?

VII. Man must first understand his role, and the part he shall fill in the bigger picture.

VIII. One thinks he knows his own purpose: but from the beginning was his purpose given unto him.

IX.   Consider the bird and how it journeys in flocks: examine the ant how it travels with brethren.

X.   Contemplate the herbs of the field how that the like grows according with its likeness.

XI.   Religion! O Religion! What art thou? But the separation and division of thy people.

XII.   Surely religion brings separation: and there is a prince of God that brings unity.

XIII.   Surely many have fallen by
religion: and by the angel of the
Lord cometh resurrection.

Chapter Three

I.   The sun shineth with all brightness: but man lurketh down a dark path.

II.   How safe are thy paths in the light, but how dangerous are thy paths in darkness: and when the snake cometh shall it be perceived, or shall ye be bit?

III.   Walk not with thine eyes: but in faith and in truth.

IV.   Illusions doth abound; for one shall run to and fro, but not unto the Lord.

V.   Wherefore do ye walk about holding thy pants? Is it not easier to walk thereto with both hands free?

VI.   Consider a maze wherein all paths lead to death save one.

VII.   A fainthearted man shall walk the straight and narrow path: but thereof doth he slip, turning to the left or the right.

VIII.   Ponder upon the straight path and strengthen thy balance.

IX.   Play the field, know thy surroundings: be unto them as a chameleon in the forest.

X.   Play thy campaign, watch thy steps: and make haste to flee these times.

Chapter Four

I.   There is a man without fear of death because he feareth God: and there is a man that feareth death because he is without wisdom.

II.   O seed of Jacob, be not fainthearted and worry not; the time shall come when the latter days exceed the present.

III.   As the man that hath plotted upon evil and so prevailed: Indeed shall he overcome that doth rest his head upon the ways of the Lord.

IV.   The rich man shall descend down into the depths of darkness: and the poor man ariseth into the light.

V.   Concerning the world, what profit hath a man that he should lose his life twice?

VI.   How pleasant is death unto the upright, and dying to the righteous? That the new man may spring forth.

VII.   Can thou who art of little faith buy his way into life? Can the rich man add one minute to his hour glass?

VIII.   Riches prevail not over death: but righteousness delivereth in the day of wrath.

IX.   Deceit compasseth the abyss: and
the wicked shall not escape the
tempest.

X.   The perfect man shall flee day
and night: but the wicked shall be
snared in the abysmal.

XI.   With the sword sinners fight for
the rich: and the righteous do
fight for the poor.

XII.   He who is poor in spirit hath
more than he whom is wealthy in
the flesh.

XIII.   And he that is poor in truth is more beautiful than he that is rich in semblance.

XIV.   Many are the days of immortality: but few are the days of mortality.

XV.   Many are the ways of mortality: but one is the way unto immortality.

XVI.   Better it was for him not to be born: than that he should perish in the midst of sin.

Chapter Five

I.   A man that hath wisdom
knoweth God: but in the mouth
of fools is blasphemy.

II.   A righteous man looks round
about and his indignation
increaseth: but the fool speaketh
things not to be spoken.

III.   Take little heed unto him whom
doth speak hatefully: as his
words are but vanity.

IV.   And when thy talk is not of
wisdom, shall it not be of
foolishness?

V. Hold thy opinion; for there will be a time when one seeketh counsel.

VI. The mouth of the unlearned speaketh out of turn: but the diligent knoweth the time and place.

VII. First seek to listen; be attentive, and therefore speak when the time is right.

VIII. By the tongue many shall be known: and by the tongue many shall perish.

IX.   There be many that mock: but few that sit alone.

X.   A wise man is not sought on behalf of his wisdom: but many ears attend unto folly.

Chapter Six

I. Together we stand tall: but divided we fall by the sword.

II. Seek not personal gain: but that of thy brethren.

III. And if thy friends are wicked, what does that say about thee?

IV. The greatest master of all is the greatest servant of all: and call no man master save God.

V.   There is a man superior to the nations: but a chain is only as strong as its weakest link.

VI.   A wise man commeth across a pot of gold and thinks upon his nation: and the fool thinketh how he can help himself.

VII.   A wise man shall labor for his brethren: and the fool laboreth for himself.

VIII.   A wise man shall labor not thinking of himself: but the fool and the sluggard shall not labor thinking of himself.

IX.   There is a man that hath many enemies: and there is one that is separate.

X.   There is a man more about his nation then himself: and there is another that strengthens the hand of the enemy.

XI.   There is a man that deceiveth his brother: and there is a brother that deceiveth himself.

XII.   There is one that decieveth himself: for blindness maketh his end obscure.

XIII.   Thy mother is who gave birth
unto thee: but God is whom
created thee.

XIV.   He whom begot thee is thy
earthly father, but God is thy
heavenly Father.

XV.   And thy family is not those with
who gave birth unto thee: but
those of whom are with the Lord.

Chapter Seven

I.   It is a sinful deed to hate thy brethren: for without them there would be no you.

II.   Reward evil with righteousness: and love those that hate thee.

III.   To know love is to know fear: and to know hate is to know love.

IV.   To love one more than another is as to hate the other: and whomever thou doth love the most, which is whom ye shall follow.

V. And to be without love is to be without fear, is to be without faith, and is to be without hope.

VI. And even when thou are hated, love thy haters as thou would love thy brother.

VII. To know evil is to know good: and without the law there would be no evil.

VIII. When evil is done unto you repay evil with good.

IX.   For love doth exceed choice silver: and charity over powers all fine gold.

X.   There is an abomination in the eyes of the Lord: and there is a man that hateth evil.

XI.   The good man rebuketh out of much love, but the evil shall blind his eye until, of course, the lot of wickedness falls upon his own head.

XII.   There is a man that seeketh love: and there is a man that loveth death.

Chapter Eight

I. Strong drink has been spread throughout the earth: but the elect shall sober up.

II. He whom hath created the heart of old, also hath power to create a new heart.

III. Can a brother rob a bank, give it to the poor and say, behold, I have done a good work?

IV. As to the liking of a snake: so is he that layeth stumbling blocks for the blind.

V.   Thy servant hath slipped and quickly sprang back upon his feet, as if a pack of wolves pursueth him: and the fool sinned saying within his heart, I deceived man and thus am in the clear.

VI.   Trust not in thy heart: for there be many deceived by folly.

VII.   Follow not thy heart: For many have been led astray.

VIII.   There is a way which is unseemly and there is a way which seems to be: but man worketh that not to be and worketh not that which should be.

IX.   That which shall come is to be: and that which is to be shall come.

X.   Lean not on thine own power, for what is thy power compared unto that of another? But instead, therefore lean on the strong arm of the Lord.

XI.   There is a man that tiptoes as a woman: and a woman that runneth as a man.

XII.   The woman that feareth God honors her lord.

XIII.   The man that feareth God honors
the Lord: and thus does Christ
unto the Father.

XIV.   If it be so, better it is for a man
not to cover his head, that honor
may shine in due time.

XV.   However, times doth change: but
as for God, he changes not.

XVI.   Surely there is a million excuses:
and for such there is a flaming
sword.

XVII.   Surely there is a million liars:
and there is walking charcoal.

XVIII.   The fool shall trespass against
the Lord ignorant of his
puissance: and the blind art near
thy estimation.

Chapter Nine

I.   He that is full of strife will end up nothing withouten: and in such presence, who will not catch ghost?

II.   And there was one of exceeding wisdom: but it was temptation that surrounded him on all sides.

III.   You can run, you can hide, and you can deceive, but where so ever you go, temptation shall be right behind thee.

IV.   Curses follow the wicked in their wickedness: and blessings are in the house of the wise.

V.   There is a brother quick to wrath, but slow is another to anger: and where there is confusion there shall be peace.

VI.   A feeble man that seeks peace is stronger than a man of might, quick to wrath.

VII.   The righteous grow stronger as a tree that taketh root: but the wicked shall disintegrate.

Chapter Ten

I. The wind covereth the face of the earth: as wisdom shall inhabit the worlds.

II. All riches are but little unto the man that hath found wisdom: and all wisdom is in the eyes of the Lord.

III. For by wisdom did he create thee: and by wisdom thou canst live forever.

IV. A hypocrite is a hard man: but wisdom is with the broken

V. A man that hath wisdom hath a great fear: as one that trembles in the night.

VI. One that seeketh wisdom shall find knowledge: and the application of the same giveth understanding.

VII. To have understanding is to have wisdom: but to have knowledge is to have the keys to perfection.

VIII. Wisdom showeth forth action: and the same shows fear of God.

IX.   Fear of God showeth forth prudence: as strength is shown in the day of adversity.

X.   A man that hath fear of God feareth evil: and the man that departs from evil understands.

XI.   Knowledge is the doctrine of immortality: and the performance of her showeth forth wisdom.

XII.   A man that hath knowledge knows evil: and he that flees from sin hath understanding.

XIII.   A man that taketh heed to the law
hath wisdom: and he that leaves
off death showeth forth
understanding.

XIV.   Knowledge goeth forth into the
ear of the upright: as morning
dew distills upon the house tops.

XV.   The truth is obscure for many:
and unto the wander in darkness
there is light.

XVI.   Light goes forth from the
heavens: as truth from the mouth
of the righteous.

XVII.   Know light by the light, as truth by the truth, as knowledge by the knowledge of God.

XVIII.   Strength cometh of understanding: and powerful is the man that departs from evil.

XIX.   There is but one truth: and they that take hold of it shall find perfection.

XX.   And this is the purgetero, the path to paradiso, through the inferno ending at Salem.

SALEM:

A City On A Hill

Chapter One

I. The Kingdom of God is likened unto a light that shall never fade away.

Chapter Two

I.   There was a tree that arose upon the face of the earth.

II.   This certain tree was likened unto wind that blows hereto there.

III.   Never knowing in which it shall be blown.

Chapter Three

I.   Thy son hath fainted, and thus fallen into deep sleep.

II.   And the evening and the morning were the first day.

III.   Time moved, the sun shifted, and the moon shone with exceeding brightness.

IV.   And the evening and the morning were the second day.

V.   Thy son awoke from sleep: the physician checked his brain, and in its place there lie the Book of Life.

Chapter Four

I.   A world on a timer is likened unto the ant kingdom.

II.   Then a certain man cometh and trodden down the kingdom.

III.   And lo, the ant looks around at his brethren.

IV.   And does he hesitate?

V. He is determined to fight for his brethren, that their glorious kingdom may be rebuilt.

Chapter Five

I.   Now there was a man born in the image, and likeness of his Father.

II.   From the beginning of his time, and since he was withdrawn from the womb, he was given the breath of life and became alive.

III.   The same begot two sons the one older than the other.

IV.   And when the sons came of age, their father departed until the time to be fulfilled that he should return.

V.   The elder son became skillful in all parables, dark sayings, and hidden proverbs.

VI.   He knew all mysteries of the times, the beginning, midst, and end of times.

VII.   Namely how the earth was formed, the flood that ravished upon it, and how the world would end.

VIII.   His fame went out round about, and he became renown among all that dwelt upon the earth.

IX.   For he waxed exceeding great
and all the kings of the earth
gave homage unto him.

X.   As for the younger son, he was a
plain man full of wisdom,
knowledge, and understanding.

XI.   He was invisible unto the world
and never sought out on behalf of
his wisdom, and by many was he
hated.

XII.   All that beheld him, and heard
the words of his tongue only
mocked, and scorned him.

XIII.   Furthermore the people said that his father would forget about him, and on behalf of his brother's greatness he would not be remembered.

XIV.   And as time passed, news reached the brothers that their father was coming home.

XV.   Thus the elder son made ready great riches and a crown of gold to place upon his father's head at whence he returned.

XVI.   And when he arrived home, the elder son approached nigh unto him first.

XVII.   And his father paused, and wondered greatly, then said unto his son, depart from me I never knew you.

XVIII.   Then came the younger son with his head down and the father ran out to meet him saying, O my beloved son how I have desired to behold thy face!

Chapter Six

I. In the land of Uz there was a man that had a court date at the court house, of which he knew not the direction.

II. And once a day for three days he was instructed to find the path.

III. The first day one came unto him saying, sir, it would behoove thee to the route, and he replied, it will be fine I will handle it.

IV. And the second day one came unto him saying, sir, needest thou not to get directions?

V.   And he replied, I will get right on it once I finish this first, but time passed by.

VI.   Lastly, on the third day a wise man came unto him saying, good sir, hath thou found thy way? And he replied, no not yet.

VII.   And the wise man replied saying, good sir came I henceforth that I might show you the way,

VIII.   And he replied, my brother it will be fine I have time, I do not need help.

IX.   The day came that man had to stand before the judge, but he never took the time to find the way and so he was late.

X.   Though he sought carefully with tears for forgiveness, the judge would not hear his words.

Chapter Seven

I.   John the sower sowed seeds in his garden, and in his garden there was not a seed that was not sown.

II.   Every year the harvest was plentiful and he had more than enough.

III.   Year by year John gave all his overage unto those of whom needed it more.

IV.   So that he had no excess, but enough that he might feed his family.

V.   Now Peter the sower and neighbor to John sowed seeds in his garden, and in his garden there was not a seed that was not sown.

VI.   Every year the harvest was bountiful and he had more than enough.

VII.   Year by year Peter heaped all his goods that he might live off the fat of his land.

VIII.   So that Peter had much excess and more than enough to feed his family.

IX.   After sundown a thief came by night and stole all their seeds that he could get his hands on.

X.   Insomuch that they had just enough to feed their families.

XI.   And when Peter saw all that befell him, his heart sank within him and he fell into depression for he had great possessions.

XII.   But John arose the next day and saw all that took place, and he looked up into heaven as if his face were the face of an angel.

XIII.   And with a loud voice spake
saying, blessed be the Lord God
of Israel.

Chapter Eight

I. In the days when the earth had grown old and the worlds become corrupt, and the thoughts of mortal men continually evil.

II. The Most High called his servant from among the simple, and chose one out of many that sought immortality.

III. God formed Jeshurun to be a warrior and of his life, to have no end.

IV. And from his youth, Jeshurun wielded his sword day and night.

V.   Insomuch, not a day went by that he did not train and meditate thereof.

VI.   Sword in hand, he was skilled in all manner of warfare and all the people marveled at his appearance.

VII.   And the young boy rose up upon the earth and when he became of age, he girded himself in the spirit.

VIII.   Straightway, Jeshurun travelled from country to country, state to state and city to city slaying evil with his sword.

IX.   For in one city he slew two
hundred, and in another he drew
his sword against five hundred,
and the slain of him were many.

X.   All his days Jeshurun fought evil
until the time to be fulfilled:
therefore that he might be
acceptable in the sight of the
Lord.

Chapter Nine

I. Blind from birth and distressed in a dark world, King Lion looked up unto the heaven of heavens as rain poured down upon him.

II. And said, O God, how that thou wouldst!

III. And in the greatness of his mercy, God revealed the Comforter unto King Lion.

IV. And lo, there appeared light out of the abyss, and King Lion received sight that he might see.

V.   And he beheld, and looked round about only to behold his kingdom trodden down and brethren destroying themselves.

VI.   Wherefore King Lion's heart failed him, and he fell upon the ground.

VII.   Therewith he thought upon the comforter, wherein God called him saying, rise up and follow me.

VIII.   Wherewith he sprang back upon his feet and pushed forward into the light.

Chapter Ten

I.   The kingdom of heaven is likened unto a certain woman who inherited and house.

II.   And it came to pass, as she attempted to enter, she found herself locked out.

III.   Though she inherited the house, she was locked out of that which was hers from the beginning.

IV.   So she called her husband, and he said, I'm coming speedily and tarry not to unlock the house, just hold tight.

V.   Therefore, until then, she searched for any entrance into her house and found herself completely locked out.

VI.   And so she arose, went to her porch, stood upon her feet and watched for her husband.

VII.   And lo, there he appeared with the key to unlock her inheritance.

Credits:

All praise to the MOST HIGH and his son Jesus the Christ.

I thank my father and mother for bringing me into this world.

Double honors to my Bishops and Deacons.

Citations:

(N. Israel, personal communication, January 2013 – January 2014).

(Y. Israel, personal communication, January 2013 – January 2014).

(I. Israel, personal communication, August 2013 – January 2014).

Resources:

Visit, www.BlacksandLatinos.net and subscribe and stay updated for future releases.

Follow me: Twitter.com/EzraMicaiah

Facebook.com/BlacksandLatinos

The Book of Salem

www.ingramcontent.com/pod-product-compliance
Lightning Source LLC
Chambersburg PA
CBHW031527040426
42445CB00009B/424